Impressions in Thought

Jocelyn Flojo

For my father, Joe, and my mother, Diana, whose unwavering encouragement began with my very first "roses are red" poem. They taught me to believe in myself and to never abandon my dreams.

Acknowledgement:

I want to express my heartfelt gratitude to my family—Dennis, for motivating me and supporting my myriad of endeavors; my children, Kevin, Kristen, Kyle, and Kobe, for constantly inspiring me with their creativity and unique talents; and to God, for His guidance and countless blessings.

Preface:

I remember, as a child, writing poems for my mom and dad. They always began with "Roses are red, violets are blue," followed by a couple of rhyming lines. I never imagined those simple verses would lead me to where I am today as a poet.

In my youth, I participated in young writers' contests and conferences, winning roses for my mom in a Mother's Day poetry contest by the local *Daily Herald* newspaper. I also submitted poems to my high school's literary magazine. Later I began college as an English major, but then—life happened. I got married, started a family, and built a career that evolved through various roles across different organizations.

Before I knew it, I was 49, going on 50. My youngest child a senior in high school, with the elder two done with college and starting their own lives. For the first time in years, I had the space to reflect on my life and return to the dream and passion for writing, and writing poems specifically, that had remained dormant for so long.

Once I started again, I found I couldn't stop. Over the years, I had written occasional poems scattered among journal entries, but I had never truly dedicated the time to explore whether my thoughts and feelings could once more take creative shape on the page—let alone be shared with others. That is, until now.

So here I am, and here is what I want to share. These words may resonate with some, spark interest in others, or be met with indifference. But please know this: every poem comes from my core, my truth, and my soul.

And now I offer these pieces of myself to you.

Buried

Burying myself in memories
Filling the holes dug each time you left.
On shallow mounds I sit
and ponder
Sheltered by leaves and
grass
Gathered and foraged
At my own will.

My mind—numbed
My heart—hollow
No thoughts of love and
longing remain,
Except for messages written long ago.
Wishing for something,
Until I become one with the land.

Encore Un Jour

Encore un jour,
Again, one day,
With sincerest regrets,
To go back to that moment
When I could have chosen joy for you.

Instead I left you hurt—
I made you sad, angry, with tears and sobs,
And all I could offer was "sorry".
Nothing else could be done.
I still go back to that time
Wishing the right decision was made,
But it wasn't.

Maybe you have forgotten,
Although I won't ask if you have...
Not wanting you to remember
That day I failed (and other times as well).

"Please forgive me."
I say each time I see you,
But only in my head.
Encore un jour, again, one day,

I'll apologize once more.

Catch a Breath

Sometimes, how foolish I am,
Allowing invasions into my soul—my spirit.
Burying myself with overthinking thoughts
Gathered within me
Feeding on my every sense.
To extremes of empathy,
Then to apathy,
No balance or in-between.
Like a slave to its will,
It leads me to places
Where I drown.
I rise for air,
Just enough to catch a breath,
Only to sink and
To tread water again.
Telling myself, over and over,
Make it to the shore,
Where sanity awaits,
Where actions and feelings make sense.
Escape the sea of mindlessness and care —
Too little mind,
Too much to bear.

Send me a raft,
A life preserver to save me...
But I know it will never come.

Casting Shadows

Casting shadows on playgrounds and parks.
Always saying, "Come home when it gets
dark."
Shadows have grown
Just as the years have flown.
To have slowed time,
If only I had known
That life is swift,
Too brief, if we're not careful.
As I see and feel now,
I reach for your hand,
And it is me that you must pull.
My core is full,
With memories of days not far behind.
My emotions are a storm within,
But to you, I cannot show.
Not wanting you to worry about me —
Not sure if you ever would.
I'll worry enough
For us both,
And go with you,
If only I could.

Traveling Through Towns

Traveling through towns,
Scenes of bygone histories past,
Mixed with the pulse of modern living,
And lives
Intertwined with generations from decades
past
To years, months and perhaps days new.
Walking past with a gentle hello,
Or maybe a wave from a familiar car driving
by.
Neighbors, friends, and strangers,
Greeting each other – or not –
Depending on the mood,
Or the hour,
Or the day.
As some rush hurriedly starting their day
While others pace ever so slow,
No need to hasten
For those who have closed that chapter
Gifted ample time
Catch up with friends at a local coffee shop

Reading the daily paper
Or well-worn book,
To absorb the characters and scenes once
more.
Life in these towns,
I pass each day,
Gazing through the window
On my morning train...
Maybe one day I'll stop,
And become one to mingle or
Make my home there.

Whole

You may look at me
And see my eyes,
You may look at me
And witness me cry.
But I am whole,
Deep down inside,
You didn't break me,
Even though you tried.
My tears aren't for you,
Or for what could've been,
They're for the person inside me,
The one who let you in.
I grieve for that soul
Who loves and gives
Without second thought
I failed to protect
This time around,
But I am whole—
Know that,
When you may look at me.

She Crosses Paths

She crosses paths
That feel familiar—
Was it in dreams?
A different time?
Too long ago to remember.

The flutter of butterflies above,
Mesmerizing in their ascent,
Wishing she could fly with them
Sunlight cascading wings
Views from high above
To see a world she sees
Only when she sleeps
Fragrant and blooming flowers,
Guiding her way.
She peers closely towards one.

Spotting a bumble bee float
From one bloom to the next
No cares, always knowing what it needs to do
She feels a faint of envy
To live carefree
"Why can't that be me?"

She crosses paths
No longer familiar,
A journey far
To someplace new.
She stops to rest,
Making space for her thoughts,
Her mind,
Her heart.
This time she will not forget.

You Were There

You were there
When I looked up,
Catching your gaze fixed on me.
You were there—
I was too nervous to talk to you,
So you held my hand instead.
You were there
To kiss me first,
Because for me, this was all so new.
You were there
To commit, to propose,
Make our love official
When no one had dared before.
You were there
Through the highs and lows,
Of us and life.
You were there—
Before, now, and always.
You are here.

Pinball Machine

Funny how someone can feed us words
Like quarters into a pinball machine,
And our thoughts ricochet wildly—
Fast, then slow,
High, then low,
Until the words cease to be fed,
And so we sit,
Silent and dark
Once again,
Until the next one comes along.

The End of the Credits

She watches movies from beginning to end —
The end of the credits,
Where people's names scroll
From one to many,
As though she could read each name that
flashes on screen.
Maybe it's because she is giving what she
cannot get for herself—
Someone to see her,
To know her,
To understand what she has invested of
herself.
Knowing that, in the end,
She is the only one who will ever know
All the ins and outs,
The details and the time
That she gives.
One day, she will understand
That she is the only one who truly matters—
To see herself,
To know herself,
To understand herself.
That is what will bring her the happiness

She seeks—
Not from the outside,
Only from within.

Nighttime Swimming

Nighttime swimming with subtle waves,
Lit only by the reflection of the moon above.
I drift silently and alone,
But not lonely—
Because this is where I want to be.
The only sound is my own breath,
Deep within the water,
So soft yet powerful.
Knowing the awe,
Not taking my Creator for granted—
Allowing me this space,
This time,
To think—or not.
To simply exist here,
A miracle in itself.
Thoughts continue to swim
Through my mind
Beneath the veil of night.

Chasing Home

I lay awake, thinking—
Why am I always chasing a place called home?
Searching for a place where I can feel
Peace,
Joy,
Calm,
Happiness,
Love.
Is it hidden somewhere out there? In a
Place,
Object,
Person?
That's when a voice whispered, "No." It is in
Me,
Faith,
God.
And that is when I stopped chasing
Home.

Where the Horizon Meets the Sky

I thought I saw you
Where the horizon meets the sky,
Your figure moving, then twirling—
A silhouette, a shadow.
Even then, I swear I could still see you smile,
Your arms reaching high, weightless, free.
Were you trying to fly?
Like an angel that had landed on earth,
To share with the world
The beauty and grace of life.
Although I know this may have only lived in
my mind,
I will always believe that I did see you
Where the horizon meets the sky.
And maybe, just maybe, you will see me too—
Come find me, visit me, even if only for a
while.

Send My Love

Send my love to the one who now loves you,
Since I could not give you more—
Or maybe I gave too much.
They see in you what I once saw,
But maybe they care a little less.
Because I couldn't (or didn't want to) see
Any blemish or improvement I thought
should be made.
I loved you fully, as you were and as you are,
But you don't want someone to love you
whole.
You want (and maybe need)
A person who will take a chisel to you,
When I wanted to mend and heal the cracks.
Send my love to the one who holds you now.

In Passing

I sat staring out the window one late
afternoon.
You hadn't noticed in passing,
So you continued on to your day —
A kiss on the cheek —
Then you went on your way.

I read a book about a far-off land,
Where life was calm and the skies were blue.
I finished it and couldn't wait to tell you
about it, but
You hadn't noticed in passing.
"See you later," you said —
And rushed out the door —
So I went back to bed.

I put on a new dress and the perfume you
bought me.
You hadn't noticed in passing.
Another appointment you had to catch —
You mustn't be late —
And there I stood, giving out a deep breath.

I packed a bag and left it by the door, still
You hadn't noticed in passing.
You gave me a hug with a smile on your face—
"We'll do something later," you said —
And left once again.
Moments later, I left as well,
To never return to that place, but
You hadn't noticed in passing.

Ripples

Why are your emotions like ripples?
Moving around and through me with highs
and lows,
A moment of tranquility,
Where peace and calm envelop me,
Until unexpectedly,
The rush of power and currents
Toss me away,
Rocking my core
Hard and with force,
Leaving me bruised and in pain.
Yet I stay,
Because my love is as deep as the water
We drift on.
I float and tread to stay above,
Where the waves subside once more.
I can take a breath,
I can close my eyes,
Stay in silence again,
Not knowing when your emotions
Will come back to take me over,
To fill my lungs,
Where I can no longer breathe,

Only to drown
And sink to the ocean floor.

Familiar Dream

With just a glance,
He looked at her,
And without a thought,
Approached her —
One he thought he knew before.
Maybe from another time,
So familiar she seemed,
As if they had known each other,
Had spoken before,
Held each other in the dark,
With the stars gazing from above,
And kissed with soft, pursed lips,
Gentle with love.
She returned the glance,
And offered her smile,
Shyly and with grace,
Because she felt the same.
The young lady held out her hand,
And he took it,
To feel the touch
Of a familiar dream
That had become reality.

Race Against Time

Your days may seem like a race against time,
When you try to outrun the ticking hands of
the watch.
Getting ahead,
Trying to compete with the seconds, the
minutes, and the hours,
Instead, it speeds up further,
The more you try to fight it.
It wears you thin,
Exhausting you and making you weary.
So you stop and rest,
You take a moment to breathe,
Inhale deeply,
Closing your eyes,
And realize that time is relentless—
It will not stop,
For you,
For anyone.
Embrace it you must,
And time, you must trust.
And in gratitude
Take each second, minute, and hour,
And no longer take them for granted.

The Ask

Remember the time when you asked me to
dance?
The silly song that a band played that night,
The one where the crowd knows all the
words,
So they sing along?
I was unsure but said yes anyway.
I couldn't even look you in the eyes,
But you understood that I was just being shy,
That I was happy you came my way.
You spun me around,
Embarrassed that I didn't even know how to
do that right.
So you put your arm on the small of my back
To steady me,
And make me feel safe.
So we danced until the end of that song,
And continued on,
Until the band stopped playing.
And you wanted one more,
So you asked — pleaded even —
For another tune to be played,
And so they did,

And so we did,
Dance until you asked me to dance
With you for the rest of our lives.

Your Shadow Remains

The room in silence,
But your shadow remains,
A reflection of you on a mirror,
I swear I saw in the corner of my eye.
But when I looked,
I only saw myself.
Awakened one night
By the sound of your voice,
Spoken in my ear.
And when I opened my eyes,
I lay alone in the dark.
The smell of you
Lingering around me,
And I breathe it in,
Hoping it stays within forever.
But as I exhale,
So does your scent.
The brush I felt
Along my skin,
I know it was your touch,
But I am alone.
You are no longer here,
Only your shadow remains.

The Steps

You once said to me
That you counted the steps to my door.
I thought it was funny,
And then you told me,
You did it to see how many
steps it would take to reach
me,
And hoped that soon
enough,
The number of steps would
get fewer and fewer,
Until you were with me
always.
And that's when I knew,
I could possibly, maybe,
Fall in love.
Even though I didn't want to.
I said I couldn't and shouldn't,
But your steps to my door
Wouldn't end,
Until eventually,
The number of steps did get fewer and fewer,
And we were together always.

A Calling

A calling that comes
From where?
I cannot tell,
But it pulls me in,
Draws me towards
What is meant to be,
Like destiny or fate—
If I dare believe.
It reveals what my life's direction is,
Pointing the way towards a path
Open and clear,
Where nothing obstructs,
Where guides lead the way
Toward my truth,
To my contentment.
A place once imagined
Has now manifested itself,
Greeting me with an introduction,
Welcoming me with an embrace,
Reassuring me that this is where I belong,
To embark on a new chapter,
A new beginning,

A life awaits anew.

31

Floating Balloons

I saw balloons floating in the sky,
The backdrop a deep lavender,
With clouds airbrushed like delicate flower
petals.
Maybe you had called out for them,
And they were released somehow,
To bring you glee and make you laugh.
I imagine you reaching out,
To grab the strings and pull them in,
And then walk away now that you have them,
Gripping tightly so they don't slip free.
The balloons are yours now,
And you won't let them get away,
Until the day they lose their air
And no longer bring you joy.
So you finally release them,
And let them fall to the ground,
Where each one continues to deflate.
So you walk away,
And leave them where they remain.

Sleepwalker

She is a sleepwalker
One who dreams while wide awake,
Imagining days in rosy hues,
Skies so blue and clouds so white.
Only the good she will see in you,
A smile remains on her face,
Even when her heart and soul
Are dealt with heavy blows.
When fear and hate begin to show,
She looks up in prayer,
To her God above.
She'll release herself to let life flow,
Accepting what is,
And knowing when to let go.
She'll wish you well,
Even when you wished her away.
She is a sleepwalker,
Where love, hope, and happiness stay.

The Sandbox

The mementos given, hidden in the sandbox
Moments in time buried away,
Until searched for or found,
With or without intention.
Brushed clean sometimes,
Sometimes not.
Other times left underneath,
Not visible or seen,
Forgotten over time,
Maybe only remembered
Suddenly, unexpectedly, or when
A word or moment
Brings back the memory.
So you look and search for it again,
In the sandbox,
To treasure and hold dear,
Or discard it once more,
To be lost once more.

The Call of the Birds

35

The morning we heard the call of the birds,
We awoke so suddenly,
Unfamiliar with the different sounds and
melodies,
So we threw open the windows and the doors,
Ventured outside to immerse ourselves,
Unique encounters and experiences,
With bright skies and sunlight
Peering through the trees and branches,
Gliding gracefully above,
Or flitting past us, each one,
Amazed in wonder.
The call of the birds waking us to rejoice,
And be grateful for the day.

Forgetting Me Seems Easy

Did you wish upon a star to make it easy
To forget?
Throw a penny over your shoulder,
In front of a fountain and hope your wish will
be granted?
How easy it seems for you to be blasé,
As if the moments we shared
Were too simple for your heart to wipe away.
I thought the last time we spoke
You shared so much of yourself in your words,
But once I was out of your sight,
I must have also left your mind.
Forgetting me seems easy,
Like a feather blown away.

Tell-tale Patches

I put together each time we spent,
A quilt of a life when you and I began.
Piece by piece,
Stitch by stitch,
A single thread connecting each one,
From first-time kisses
To hours lost
Happy events,
And heartbroken moments too.
Each patch representing a day, a month,
And growing more and more through the
years.
Tell-tale patches of two lives becoming one,
Growing deeper as moments of our love
continue.

Just Whisper

Just whisper, you told me,
When I gleefully called your name in the
theater,
Laughter and joy dancing in my belly.
To be with you in that moment,
Sneaking out of work early,
Like misbehaving youths,
To catch an early matinee—
Carefree,
Without a care or worry,
Just to be that way again.
But now, only captured in my mind,
Living like a movie
In my memory.

Soulmate

So familiar you are to me,
Once upon a time,
A dream or passerby, perhaps by chance.
Safe and comfortable in your presence,
Still unsure if this is where we're meant to be,
Entwined in each other,
Not wanting to say "love."
But why does it feel even more than that?
Even when we are separated by distance,
You still feel near.
I know when you are thinking of me,
And I know when you have forgotten,
But you still come around,
With thirst and hunger,
For what you cannot find elsewhere,
Though you have tried.
But I linger in you,
Like you float around me.
Will this last a lifetime, or even beyond?
Attached, then detached,
To come together again (always)
Soulmates we seem.

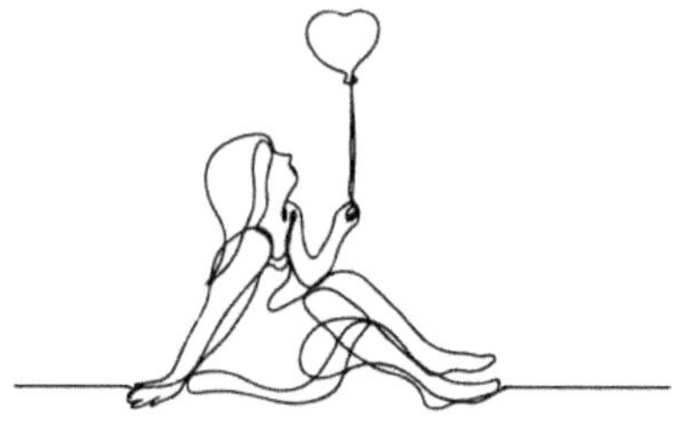

Retracing Thoughts

I retrace thoughts
Of long-ago moments,
On a timeline,
Still feeling as if they occurred just yesterday.
A time machine in my mind,
Evoking emotions long kept in my heart,
Until now.

Once again,
Retracing the thoughts
Of events that made me happy,
Content to have been there.
So simple then,
Now preserved in my memories.
So I retrace thoughts,
To feel that way once more.

Standing Back

Stand back and take a breath
Count to ten.
Know your limits,
(Or defy limits).
Pause and be still,
Clear your mind,
Release yourself.
You are here.
No need to rush,
Have faith,
Just trust.
You are blessed.
Are you ready?
Now, embrace life.

Unknowing to Know

Unknowing yet to know,
To learn who I am,
Who I can be.
Not wanting to hold steady—
One spot,
One pace,
One space,
Ever evolving,
Towards something
Beyond me now,
But taking time to understand how.
Making these goals attainable,
Until I've reached each summit,
Knowing there is no true peak,
Because there are many.
Unknowing, but now knowing,
Taking each step forward,
Once again.

Witness

They chatter about her,
But not for her.
Their lives are varied,
But still, the same.
They speak of...
Travels during breaks,
A new roommate (hoping it works),
A new job (more money and perks),
A new love (one of many but this time, the
ONE),
A child, a birthday, retirement, and the
weekend.
She is witness to their professions and
confessions,
As she sips her coffee, observes, and waits.
Another day, but never the same—
One more minute.
Her break will be over soon.

In Giving

At once, I thought to give,
But didn't.
I can only give to myself,
To God,
To those who care,
Honestly,
Authentically,
Without expecting anything in return.
As I give, without wanting or anticipating,
I give with love and care,
But careful now—
Less trusting of false intentions,
Even those unintentionally placed.
No more expectations,
Of others or myself.
Sincerity and humility remain,
As they should—
Holding hands with honesty,
To myself,
To and for God,
In giving myself whole.

Fast Lanes

Speeding in a rush
Fast lanes exist
In minds and actions,
Without thought—
Justifying carelessness and apathy,
Selfishness and fleeting satisfaction,
Temporary fixes for a pang or pain,
Hurting others and ourselves
Until we have gone too far,
Moved too fast,
And crashed.
Picking up the pieces to rebuild,
To fix and heal,
Moving now at a slower pace,
Careful with care,
And we move over,
Slower, trying not to get hit,
Or run over.
Make an exit, and slow down—
At the starting line, to begin again.

Puddle Reflections

A single drop of rain
Slinks slowly down
Plastic-framed lenses,
Amidst the hazy gray,
Seeing shadows move ahead,
Ducking in and out,
Velvet tufts of air like shrouds.
One foot in front of the other,
Every so often onto puddle reflections,
Broken by each stride.
This autumn day,
As winter looms near,
Making my way home,
Where warm light and air
Wait to embrace me.

Illustrious Illusion

He was fixated somehow
On the illustrious illusion
Watching others get accolades easily
In a glass silo, reaching out,
Wanting a taste or a touch of the sparkle and
shine,
The gold star on a piece of paper or a plaque.
Comparing to compare,
To bring himself the defeat,
For days, months, and years.
It is this illustrious illusion
That he clings to,
Not realizing the star is an ember inside,
Hidden until he discovers it,
And shifts focus inward, not outward.
Until that ember ignites and grows,
Flames on its own, breaking through the
glass,
Where he beams brightly,
On his own accord.

Steady Hands

Steady hands were held
When love was new,
Fingers intertwined, never letting go,
Savoring moments,
The touch of fingertips,
Where one begins and leads to the other's,
Security and trust,
Knowing that neither will release,
Holding each other up,
Even when standing strong,
The bond between, becoming one and
connected,
With steady hands.

Absolution

Interference and distractions,
Meandering through without consequence,
Going in directions but directionless,
Slowly veering off center and off-track,
Ever so slightly, until you are no longer
moving straight ahead,
Careening toward a wayward life
To a fleeting moment – only temporary,
When you find yourself suddenly alone and
stranded.

So you pray harder than before

Faith and hope murmur,
And you tread your way back,
Seeking God's guidance,
With remorse and humility,
Offering penance and sacrifice,
Patience as you progress,
Until you receive what you have been waiting
for—
Absolution.

Air of Gravity

The air of gravity,
Heavy and invisible,
Encapsulating, overtaking,
Feeling faint,
Out of breath,
Unsure and anxious,
Confusion lingers,
Dropping to the floor,
Collapsing like a house of cards.
A slight tremble,
Or wisp of wind,
Suddenly, a touch of grace on a shoulder,
Warmth spreading in your
chest,
Peace settling within.
Cinder blocks shattered
into dust,
A deep breath heaved,
Rising again,
Arms outstretched to
touch the weightless air,
You are saved.

Mind Games

The games that tumble inside,
Confusing truth and reality,
With illusion and façade.
Dopamine for an impermanent fix,
A high in a surreal existence,
Pretend in pretense,
Unrecognizable to yourself,
A masquerade in a fabricated ballroom
Of your mind.
Until glass shatters
And mirrors crack,
Spinning out of control,
Tripping over your own feet,
Like crumpled paper kicked to the corner,
Immovable and silent.
Tears become whispers,
Until sunlight infiltrates the stained glass,
And you lie bare to truths,
Becoming yourself again,
Humble and authentic,
Where true happiness springs,
And faith carries you forward,

Leading the way.

The Win

53

Capture and bounce,
Hit back and forth,
Stay in the game,
Eyes fixed on the ball,
Focus with all your might.
Points must be made,
One more win
Is all you need.
That is what you say,
Knowing you will crave more.
Once is never enough,
Playing to win,
Victory until it hurts.

The Scene

Laughter on lumpy couches,
Buried in blankets and oversized pillows,
Warmth emanates from close-knit bodies,
Enveloping each other in heat,
A weekly tradition of familiar films,
Projected on screens in the dark,
Yearning to preserve this moment,
Fixated on every sound, sight, and scent
Senses anchored here,
Where contentment is constant
And memories endure.

With Grace

Once I thought I could foretell the future,
Seeing what life was supposed to be.
Not even in daydreams
Was it perfect,
Abundant and bright nonetheless.
Missteps and mistakes were made,
A stumble, a fall—
Balancing myself back up,
Arms extended to the side,
Like a trapeze artist on a high wire,
Until I make it safely across,
To glimpse what's to come,
With good intention.
With grace, I forgive myself
When expectations remain unmet,
Hoping others will do the same,
Trusting that it will unfold.

Daily Walks

Daily walks up and down the streets,
Where crowds shuffle, heavy footsteps,
Early at dawn to reach their spaces,
Looking from above, high and wide.
Noise of traffic from cars and buses
Muffles the chatter of passersby.
It matters not, as music echoes
Through headphones snug against their ears,
Keeping them warm and shielded from the
wind.
Looking towards the sky
To see flocks of pigeons
Foraging crumbs and fallen food,
Ducking when a few get too near.
Not minding the daily grind,
As long as the paycheck clears.

In Defeat

Sitting there in defeat,
Surrendering to the weight of feelings,
Unforgiving in this moment,
Aware of actions that have been taken,
Confessing and acknowledged,
Accountable, filled with remorse.
Prayers yearning to be answered,
Spoken in repetition throughout the day,
Until memorized in mind and heart.
Tearful at times, more often than not,
Reaching out for a hand,
To hold and grasp,
To raise you up,
And carry you over shoulders
To a place where you can heal,
To find peace in body and spirit.
Until then, defeat you hold near.

Friday Night

Melodic twists and turns
Vibrate through the gauzy air.
Clinking glasses and bottles
Punctuate in ears over conversations
Anticipation fills the evening,
To enjoy libations poured generously,
Over translucence — frozen cold.
Excitement stirs within,
With every new greeting,
With each arrival.
Embrace and kiss,
Hands held and laughter shared,
Another Friday night,
Yet unlike the others,
Something and someone new,
Transforms the scene.

Shatter Proof

59

Not wanting to be cautious,
Filling shelves and hanging frames
With shatterproof menagerie.
No more broken glass to sweep,
Or skin to bandage from cuts.
Bubble wrap and bumper guards
For safety's sake, around the home,
Cautious and slow,
Be aware, stay vigilant.
No room for error or recklessness—
You have been there before,
No returning now.
Vault and shield what is loved,
No longer to be taken for granted.

Wax Poetic

Wax poetic on blank pages,
In a notebook discovered, tucked on a shelf,
Leaving traces of memories
Not wanting to be forgotten (or maybe you
do)
Feelings that hit you
A blow to the chest,
A punch to the heart,
And yet you record it all,
For another day to read — though unlikely.
For now, a release, an exhale,
The way to begin anew,
To start over by putting pen to paper,
Then to shut it out, leaving it in the dark,
So you can see the sun again.

Curtains Drawn

Curtains drawn to shut the day,
The sun rising to offer its greetings,
Met by cloaks on window panes,
Hiding those preferring a deep slumber,
Beneath cotton sheets and weighted blankets.
Only for those who paid no heed,
Do the cracks permit piercing light
In darkened rooms,
Glaring even to tightly shut eyes,
Wanting to crawl beneath,
To knock on doors and perform its dance,
Until they begin to awaken,
Albeit grudgingly,
To pull the curtains wide open.

Aftershock

Earth moving beneath me,
The rumble of sounds bellow,
Fragile items tremble and chatter,
Vibrations at my feet
Holding myself steady
As I make my way through,
The ripples of the ground trembling,
The aftershock from the massive quake—
Real or imagined,
Shock and surprise from the fault,
I am the one to blame.

Open Spaces

Dreaming of open spaces,
Where flower petals of peonies glisten,
Under sheer rays of sunlight,
From radiant azure skies.
Majestic clouds, painted
With feathered brushstrokes,
Walking barefoot on lush grass,
Soles and toes damp from morning dew,
Air fresh with warmth,
Embracing my body
And caressing my face.
Smiling slightly outwardly and in
Alone but not,
Without worry or care.

Never Quite Maybe

64

Never quite maybe,
The response in my mind,
Indecision,
No precision,
Never sure,
Always uncertain,
Not a definitive answer,
No affirmation or confirmation,
Commitment to decision falters,
Never quite maybe,
Most likely a no,
But who knows?

Two Way Mirror

Looking at myself,
A reflection,
But not quite me,
A two-way mirror,
My reality glaring from the other side,
A stranger to myself,
Not the same as I was,
Incremental and subtle,
Changing in nuanced gradation,
Unknowing deterioration,
Until realization from others
Breaks the trance,
Shatters the mirror,
My true self revealed,
And frees me from the masquerade.

La Vie

Cafes line cobblestone streets,
Laughter, a chorus with the music playing in
the air,
Windows frame exquisite wares and antique
art,
Vendors selling trinkets and souvenirs,
Couples walk with hands entwined
Like vines laced along garden walls,
Roses reaching out in splendor,
Greeting visitors and locals alike,
Postcard scenes in reality
Surreal in reality,
No longer a painting in a museum tour,
Basking in the city of lights,
A dream now in existence.

Rescue Myself

A rush from within,
Pushing me forward,
To somewhere unseen,
But knowing I must go,
To save myself.
Escaping the thick air,
And outreached branches,
That long to claim me and
Plant me in the ground,
Where soil crumbles
And nothing blooms.
So I move ahead,
Swiftly, almost gliding,
Feet lifted from the earth,
Dashing towards the glow,
Where life thrives,
Anything is possible,
For me and for anyone
Who opens themselves up,
Belief in letting go,
Trusting in One,
With all my faith,

With all my devotion.

Metronome Beat

Listening intently,
Laying on your chest,
Hearing the metronome beat,
Aligned with the ticking watch.
As the sound and warmth of breath
Wraps around me in security,
I feel assured of protection.
Arms enfold me,
Falling into you
Deeper into a slumber
Into a dream
Mimicking this moment
Time is motionless,
When I awaken,
And you are still here.

Incandescence

Emotions taking over,
The incandescence of beings
Brighten with strength,
Overlaying one on top of the other
In magnitude, effervescent.
Protons moving back and forth,
Each time with greater energy and force,
Striving to break through shields
Built through time,
Neither yielding
Holding to a magnetic field,
Gaining force,
Impenetrable now,
Remaining intertwined,
Bonding in permanence,
Indefinitely into infinity.

Being Human

A lesson learned,
Leaving burns,
Bruised knees,
Scarred legs,
Cover them up,
Hide them now,
Your faults and blemishes—
No one needs to know.
Losing grace,
Unforgiving toward yourself,
Prayers to a forgiving God,
Penance and remorse,
In time, forgiveness will come,
Humility and reconciliation,
For peace to fill
This space of humanity.

Glares of Clarity

Blurred glass you look through
Pervasive shadows spread throughout,
Trying to comprehend and make sense
Of those that surround you.
Wolves in sheep's clothing,
Adorn you with air-blown kisses
And veiled pleasantries—
Seemingly kind, and perhaps they are,
But push too near,
Within a hand's breadth,
Pull the red cloak over you,
Dash among the trees,
Hide and seek safety,
Expand the distance,
Until you can see with clarity,
Glaring at you with truths
You denied or ignored.
Finding shelter, you are safe now,
They can't find you here.
Lenses and panes made clear.

Dawn in Fragments

Peer through blinds,
Light refracting through,
Onto white sheets with legs stretched
beneath.
Peace and quiet on a weekend morn,
When the sounds of finches echo from above,
Finding a home from their winter escape
Wanting to live in this moment—
Just a temporary reprieve—
A break from alarms,
Dogs barking in neighborhood yards.
Knowing what it is you miss:
Little hands rustling in your wake,
Tiny eyes looking at you for comfort
Children all grown,
That dawn lives in a fragment (like many
others)
In memory.
Sleep a little longer,
As those images drift you back to slumber.

Asking for Nothing

You asked me what I wanted
When I gave you an embrace.
I ask for nothing,
Just to have you here.

I shared a smile with you,
Upon seeing your face.
Yet not trusting me,
You didn't return the smile,
Turning your back,
I felt out of place.

I wanted to tell you I miss you,
I wished to tell you how my love remains,
But I hold back for now,
Fear of rejection
Pierces me with pain.

I try to forgive myself,
And pray to God for the same.
Your forgiveness is what I wait for—
Even just a taste.

Placation

Actions speak
Not words that tumble clumsily,
Thoughts in disarray,
Not making sense in explanation
Or in decision.
Time...only time,
You tell me,
Healing wounds that leave scars.
We will ignore them
And hope they fade away,
Making new memories,
Starting over,
Forgiving one another,
Learning more
How to trust again,
Double the efforts,
Reconnecting the ties,
Binding them tightly,
So they cannot be loosened again.

Spin

Fables told in roundabout ways,
Twisting words as your head spins,
Telling tales to make your truths,
Speaking volumes without a megaphone,
Until others believe,
And you begin to as well.
Fallacies like patches on a Girl Scout vest,
That you wear all day,
Crafting fiction in reality,
Existing in hallucination,
Until the bubble bursts.

Falling Star

Gazing above to cobalt blue,
Palms open,
Arms reaching high,
Catching stars as they fall.
The moon, a magnifying glass,
A glowing pupil,
Watching over,
Guarding and observing
Every movement made,
On a quiet night—
Still and silent,
As souls sleep,
Drowsy beneath the midnight sky.

Handle without Care

Unsteady steps on gravel pavement,
Balancing fine China on fingertips,
Glass in cardboard boxes, sans bubble wrap,
Shipped and placed on the edge of a top shelf.
No care or concern of fragility.
No tiptoeing to be made,
Nor caution tape to warn.
Guardrails removed,
Free to fall—and free-falling,
To depths too deep and too far to see,
Where it stops, and where it ends,
Shattering on impact.
The safety net pulled from underneath.

Altered State

Transformation in increments
Slightly over time
Like copper turning to brass–
A shine that tarnishes,
The purity and naïveté,
Washed away beneath waves
That pull you under
And transform you to something new,
Unrecognizable now,
Your reflection in shallow water—
Even ripples recoil in shudder.
An altered state,
A sand sculpture
Crumbles down,
Exposed to the elements.

Afterthought

Never an afterthought,
Authentic and sincere,
Emotions real from the start,
Knowing the unknown,
From deep within,
A warmth from the heart,
Connecting souls that became bound
Instantaneously — not even catching a breath.
That rush and high,
A surprise, so hurried yet familiar all the
same.
Will it last forever?
Neither knowing,
But each one remains.

Cruise Control

Set yourself on cruise control,
Stay the course within the lanes,
No need to step on the gas or accelerate,
Steering unnecessary.
Keeping hands off the wheel,
Brake and pause,
Every so often,
When obstructions come too close,
Too near — making you uneasy.
Avoid the impact,
Leave it to God,
Trust your Creator,
Guiding you to follow.
Hope and belief fill you,
Faith in Him grows to each measure.

Open Fences

A fence lining the perimeter,
Around you and your heart,
Your soul guarded,
Built through time
Days of hurt and pain,
Imagined and not,
From within and without.
Wishing the posts were higher,
Invasion impossible,
Indestructible and out of touch.
Until a spark ignites out of a dark corner,
Unexpectedly, growing into a beam,
Anew with warmth, an ember of hope,
Lighting the way along the border,
Creating an opening,
Breaking through and breaking free.
A light spirit envelops you,
Embraces from within,
Peace and calm make their
entrance,
And the walls fall in their
passing.